AF334698

Carolyn Kyle

presents

Glass Patterns in Color

CKE-77

CKE Publications
Olympia, Washington

Stained Glass Friends,

Each design in this book is available as a full-size pattern. Please see the last three pages for size and source information.

The Bonus Section provides six extra patterns which are already full-size and ready to go. They will be quick to make with relatively few pieces. Extra borders are provided to change the size and look of each.

I sincerely hope that our collection of over one hundred colorful windows will be an inspiration to stained glass artists and hobbyists alike. I would like to think that it will trigger new designs, new glass uses, and new color ideas and that it will be the starting point of many windows yet to come.

Please note that many of the designs are by my associates, **Randy DeMello**, **Jackie Estes**, **Christopher Martin** and **Jan Schrader**. Credits are given to these fine artists by each of their designs.

Copyright © CKE Publications, 1986.
2030 N. Milroy St., Olympia, WA 98502
ISBN 0-935133-07-0

Copyright © Jackie Estes and Christopher Martin, 1985. Covers all Estes and Martin actual designs used in this publication.

ALL RIGHTS RESERVED. No part of this publication may be reproduced, stored in a retrieval system, or transmitted in any form or by any means electronic, mechanical, photocopying, recording or otherwise, without the prior permission of the copyright owner.

DISTRIBUTION:

CKE PUBLICATIONS
2840 E Black Lake Blvd.
Olympia, WA 98502

(206) 352-4427

CKE-11
Lake Scene
Carolyn Kyle

CKE-12
Nature's Beauty
Carolyn Kyle

CKE-55
Sailboat Window
Martin & Estes

CKE-41
Roses and Butterflies
Carolyn Kyle

CKE-45
Fruit Medley
Carolyn Kyle

CKE-67
Orchids
Martin & Estes

CKE-11
Sweet Bouquet
Carolyn Kyle

CKE-43
Gladiola
Carolyn Kyle

Narcissus

Iris

CKE-1
Flower Duet
Carolyn Kyle

Morning Glory

CKE-42
Hummingbird Duet
Carolyn Kyle

Fuchsia

CKE-9
Birds with Roses
Carolyn Kyle

CKE-16
Wagon Wheel
Carolyn Kyle

CKE-24
Mare and Foal
Carolyn Kyle

CKE-33
Farm Scene
Carolyn Kyle

CKE-80
Vegetable Banquet
Randy DeMello

CKE-21
Geese
Carolyn Kyle

CKE-88
Pig Jig
Randy DeMello

CKE-87
Rooster Reveille
Randy DeMello

CKE-86
Ducks in a Row
Randy DeMello

Frog Prince

Sittin' Pretty

CKE-75
Baby Unicorn
Randy DeMello

CKE-95
Country Cousins
Jan Schrader

This pattern can be separated and built
as a set of four 10½'' x 9'' panels.

Carousel Horse

CKE-96
Joy Rides
Jan Schrader

Rocking Horse

CKE-91
Cuddle Up Bears
Randy DeMello

CKE-74
Crescent Moon
Randy DeMello

CKE-68
Calico and Tulips
Randy DeMello

CKE-92
C'Mon Out
Randy DeMello

CKE-35
Feline Friends
Carolyn Kyle

CKE-47
Iris Scene
Carolyn Kyle

CKE-23
Koala Bear
Carolyn Kyle

CKE-38
Mountain Lion
Carolyn Kyle

CKE-48
Close-up
Carolyn Kyle

CKE-98
Columbine and Friend
Jan Schrader

CKE-32
Winter
Carolyn Kyle

CKE-64
Love Bird
Martin & Estes

CKE-76
Frick 'n Frack
Randy DeMello

CKE-56
Bamboo Window
Martin & Estes

CKE-54
Bamboo and Calla Lilies
Martin & Estes

CKE-79
Floral Bowl
Randy DeMello

CKE-69
Rosebud Vase
Randy DeMello

CKE-65
White Lilies
Martin & Estes

Note: Lines on pattern may vary slightly from photograph.

CKE-85
Budding Beauty
Carolyn Kyle

CKE-63
Arched Floral
Martin & Estes

Triple Flower

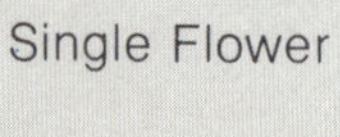

Single Flower

CKE-40
Birds and Flowers
Carolyn Kyle

CKE-22
Bird and Flower
Carolyn Kyle

Note: Photograph of window has been cropped slightly.

CKE-7
Triple Tulips
Carolyn Kyle

CKE-57
Fleur-de-lis
Martin & Estes

CKE-51
Mini Victorians
Carolyn Kyle

CKE-93
Calla Lily
Randy DeMello

CKE-52
Formal Flower
Carolyn Kyle

CKE-29
Lilies
Carolyn Kyle

CKE-58
Bird and Flower
Martin & Estes

CKE-46
Garden Prize
Carolyn Kyle

CKE-26
Pheasant in Flight
Carolyn Kyle

CKE-61
Eagle in Flight
Martin & Estes

CKE-5
Classic Silhouette
Carolyn Kyle

CKE-30
Sunny Daffodil
Carolyn Kyle

Male Mallard

Female Mallard

CKE-19
Mallards in Flight
Carolyn Kyle

CKE-17
Desert Sunrise
Carolyn Kyle

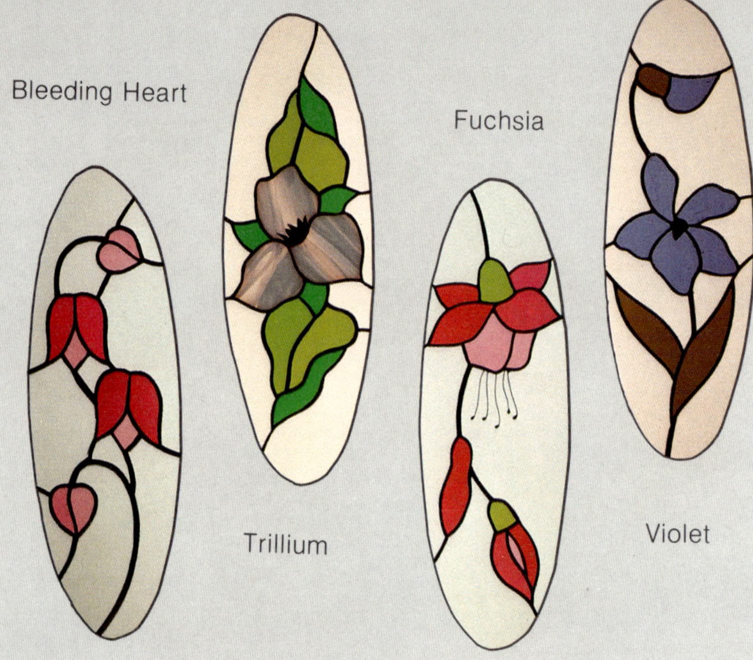

CKE-3
Flower Quartet
Carolyn Kyle

CKE-82
Orchid
Randy DeMello

CKE-10
Dogwood and Hummingbird
Carolyn Kyle

CKE-25
Horse with Branches
Carolyn Kyle

CKE-34
Enchanted Tree
Carolyn Kyle

CKE-37
Peeking Through
Carolyn Kyle

CKE-36
Bear Fishing
Carolyn Kyle

CKE-15
Deer Portrait
Carolyn Kyle

CKE-60
Deer Window
Martin & Estes

CKE-28
Fish Jumping
Carolyn Kyle

Dolphin

Whale

CKE-20
Dolphin and Whale
Carolyn Kyle

CKE-4
Driftwood
Carolyn Kyle

CKE-70
Whale
Randy DeMello

CKE-18
Sunrise on the Pond
Carolyn Kyle

Spinnaker

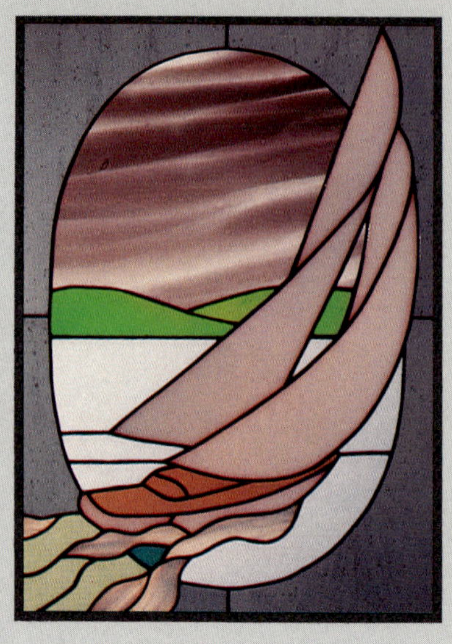

Jib

CKE-13
Sailboat Duet
Carolyn Kyle

CKE-6
Hot Air Balloons
Carolyn Kyle

CKE-94
Bird of Paradise
Randy DeMello

CKE-83
Parrot
Randy DeMello

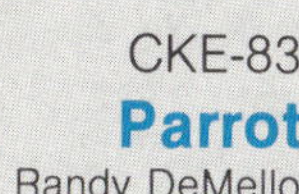

Gridwork Elegance
Martin & Estes

CKE-53
Circle Floral
Martin & Estes

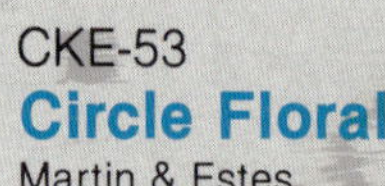

Dogwood

CKE-2
Butterfly Duet
Carolyn Kyle

Roses

CKE-59
Grape Oval
Martin & Estes

CKE-8
Rose Bouquet
Carolyn Kyle

CKE-77
Roller Balloons
Randy DeMello

CKE-39
Unicorn with Rainbow
Carolyn Kyle

CKE-73
Castle in the Clouds
Randy DeMello

CKE-72
Prancin' Fancy
Randy DeMello

Bubbles

Waves

CKE-27
Frog on Mushroom
Carolyn Kyle

CKE-66
Dancer
Martin & Estes

Mermaid

Tulips with Border

BONUS SECTION PROJECTS

Full-size patterns provided
on the following pages.

Tulips with
Butterfly

Daffodil

Puffin

Country Chicken

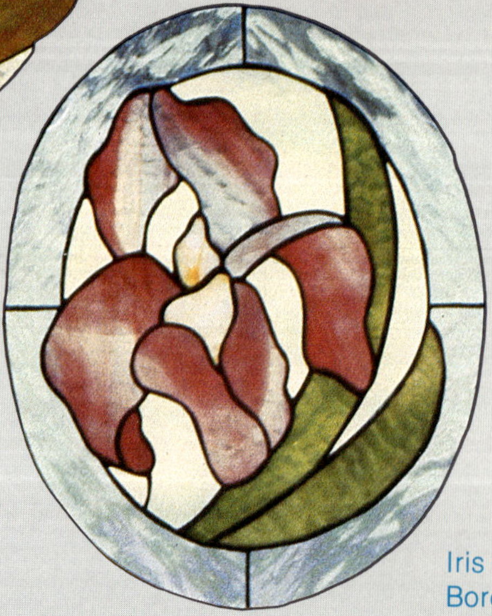

Iris with
Border

48

BONUS SECTION PROJECTS

The previous pages may well provide days and days of contemplation, idea gathering, and project planning. In the meantime, here are some smaller designs that are ready to go. They are quick to make, a good use of leftover glass, and a very nice size for gifts. Extra borders and glass add-ons multiply the different looks which can be created from the basic ovals and circles.

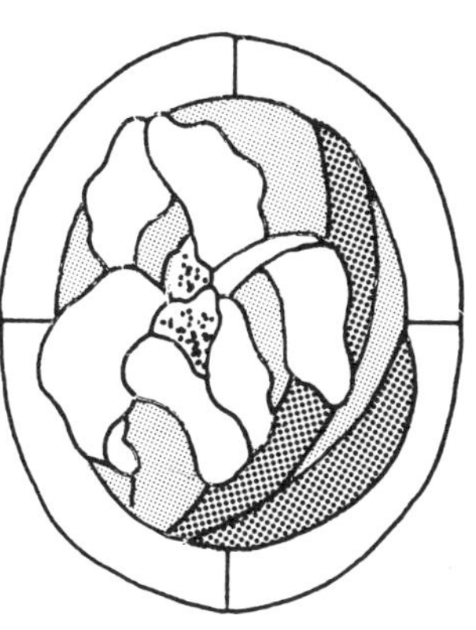

FAST AND ACCURATE PATTERN PIECES

We do not recommend using the actual book pages for the pattern. Tracing the pattern onto other paper would leave everything intact (including the pattern on the backside) for use some other time.

For even faster and more accurate results, try this:

1. Photocopy two copies of the pages to be used.

2. With scissors, cut the edge off of each pattern on the dotted line.

3. Spray the back of one set of copies with spray adhesive. Stick them to a piece of pattern paper with the cut edges touching one another and so the perimeter lines exactly match.

4. Cut through both layers, using regular scissors for the outside perimeter and then lead or foil shears for all inside pattern lines.

5. Tape together the second set of copies with transparent tape. Use this as a layout sheet on which to build the project.

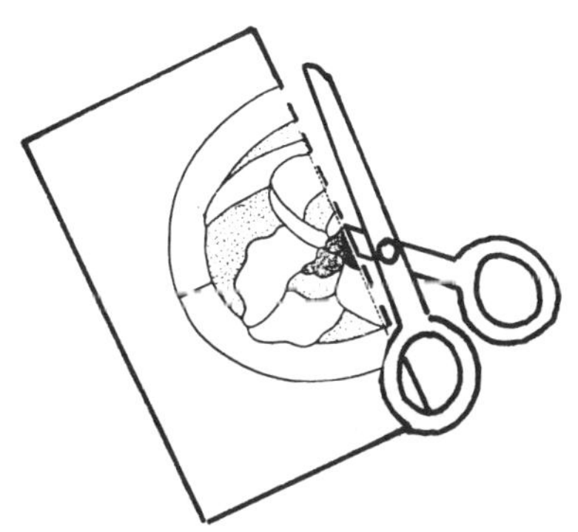

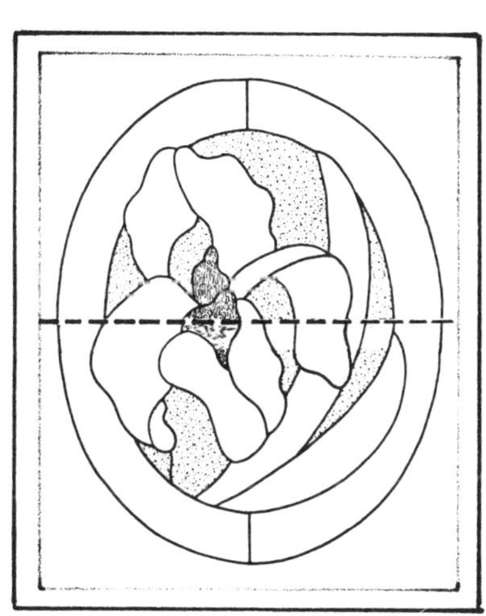

DAFFODIL

Only 22 pieces to make this cheery "Hello" for a friend. Other background glass sug-
gestions: Clear heavy textures, streakies such as yellow, orange, blue, or solid blue.

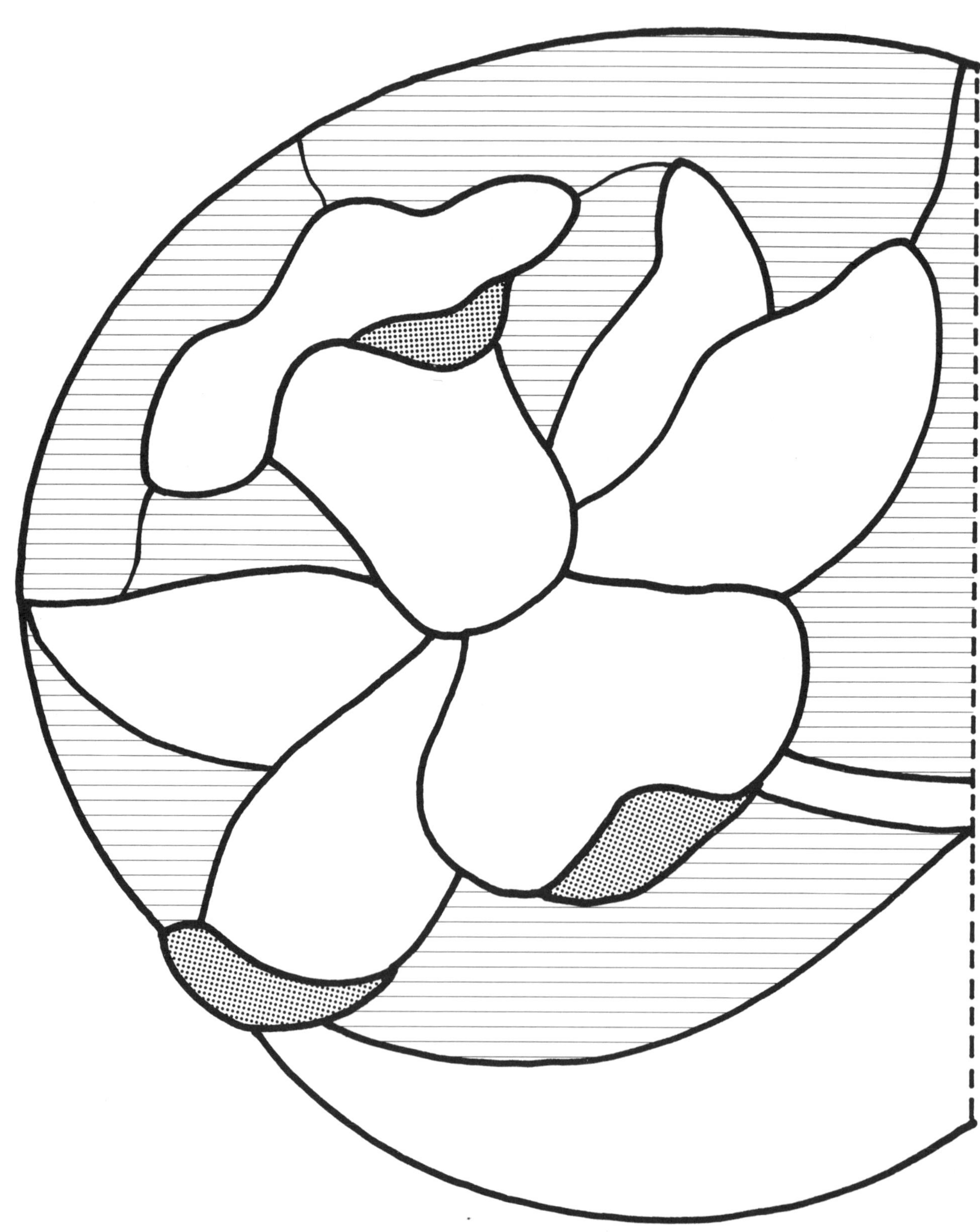

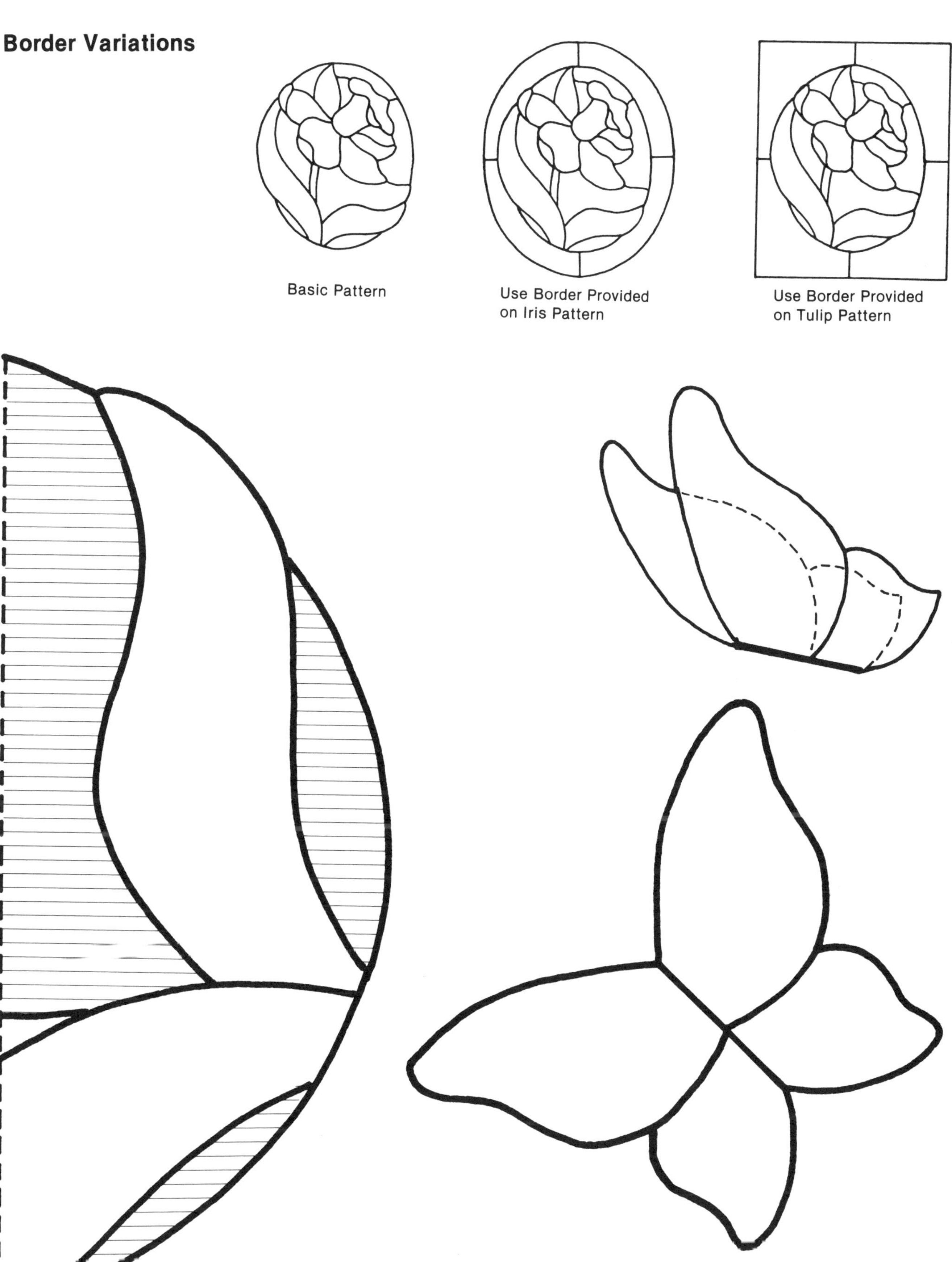

Border Variations

Butterflies

These three-dimensional cuties are a unique addition to Daffodil, Tulip, or Iris. To make, complete wings for each side of butterfly. Then with center edges touching one another at an angle, solder body line. Position on panel anywhere the butterfly body will cross two solder lines. Tack-solder to panel at these two spots.

IRIS

This lush blossom has 20 pieces without the border, 24 with.
A great opportunity to use exotic purples, blues, richly streak-
ed multi-colors, and a lot of imagination.

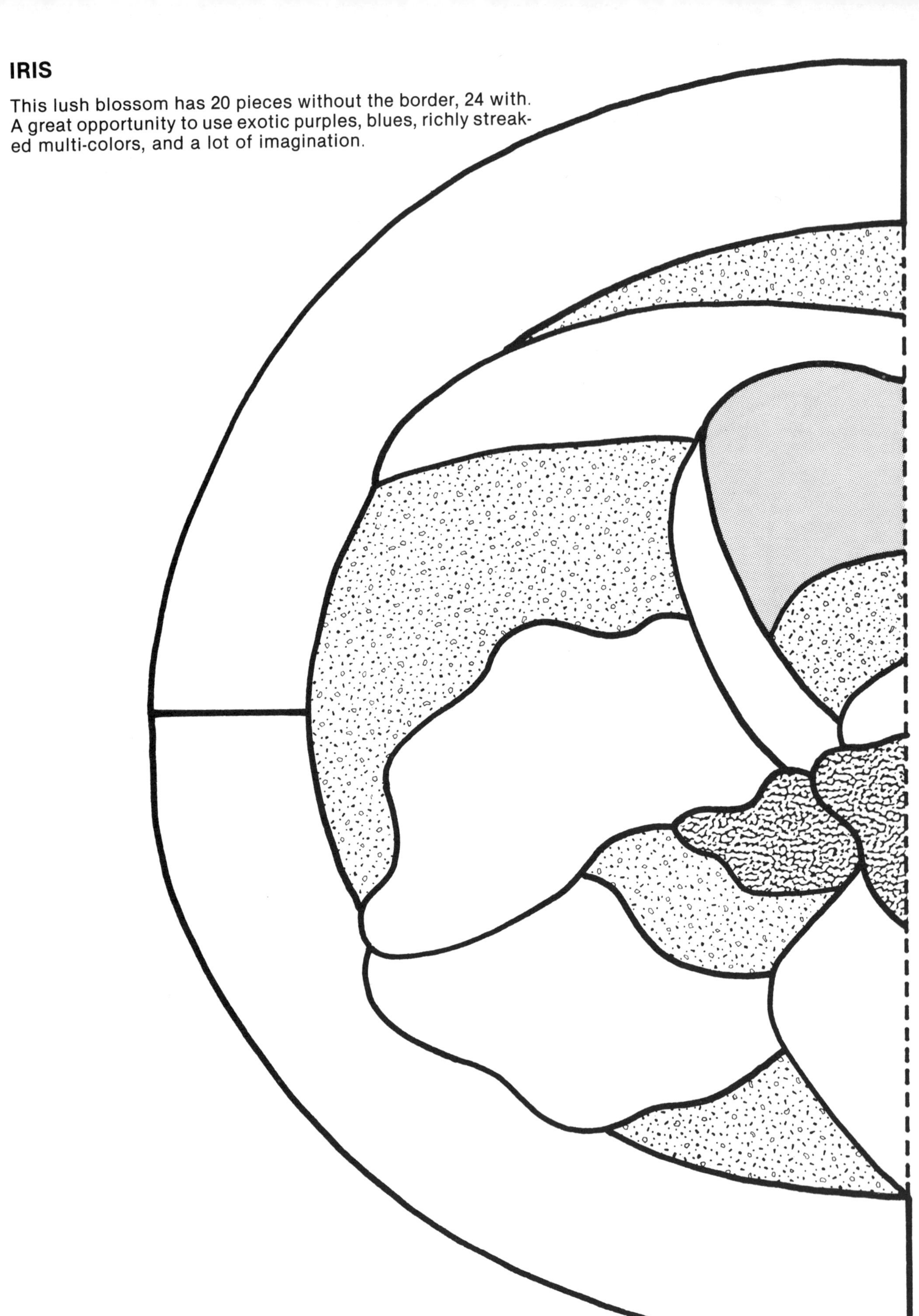

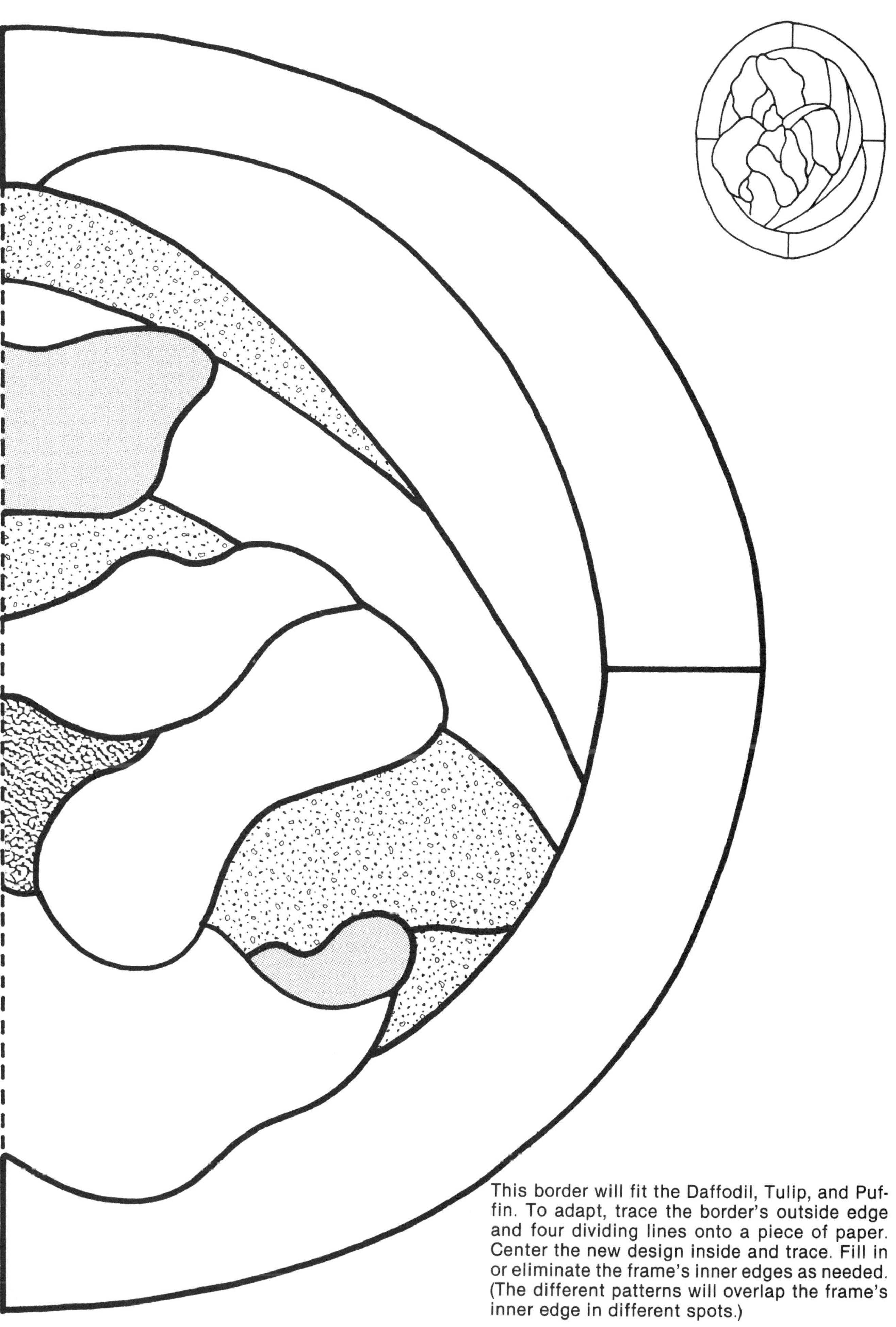

This border will fit the Daffodil, Tulip, and Puffin. To adapt, trace the border's outside edge and four dividing lines onto a piece of paper. Center the new design inside and trace. Fill in or eliminate the frame's inner edges as needed. (The different patterns will overlap the frame's inner edge in different spots.)

TULIP

There are 21 pieces in this basic tulip pattern, 25 when the border is added. A butterfly or two makes a nice addition to the tulips. (Page 51). Colors? Bright and beautiful!

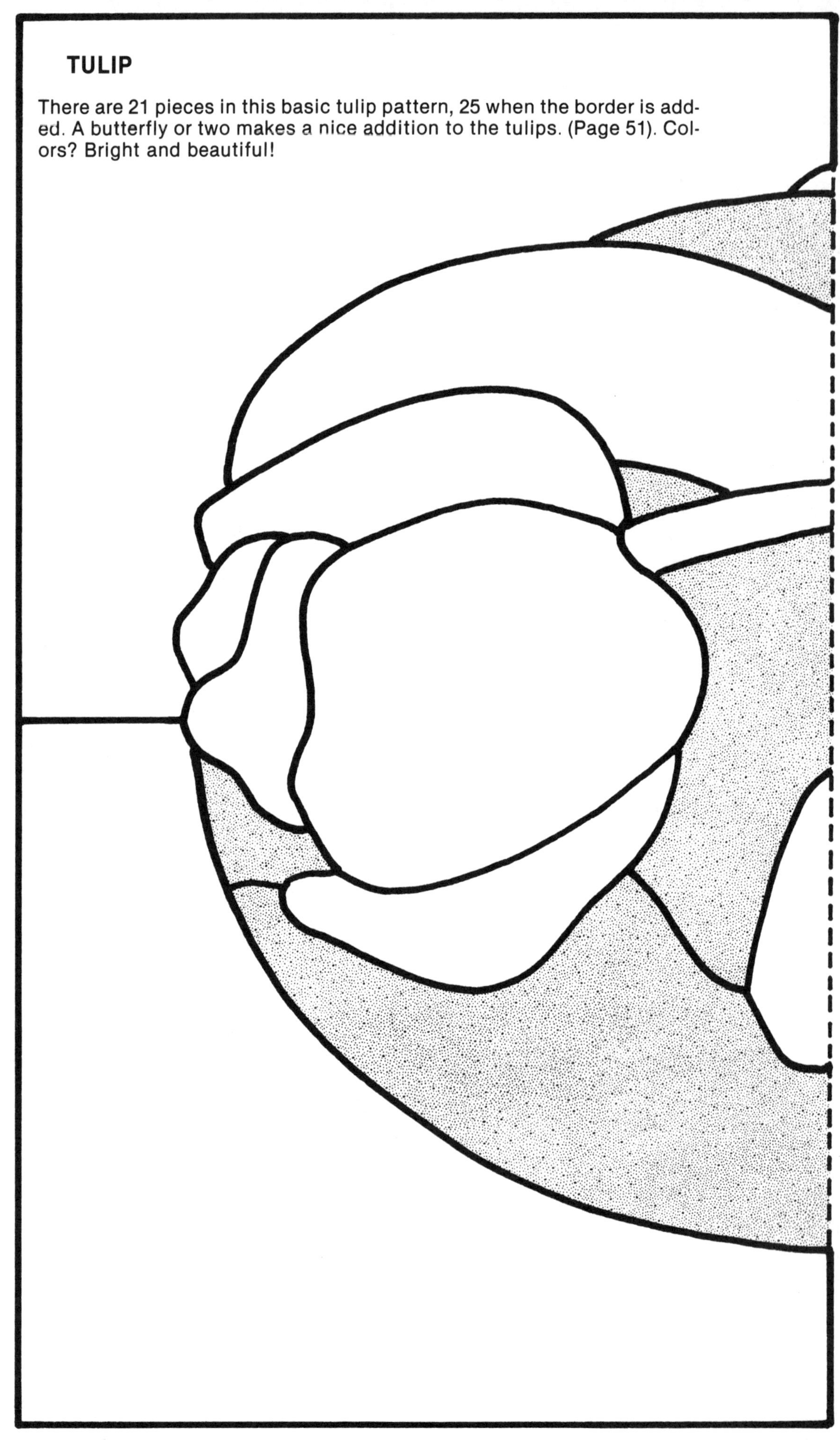

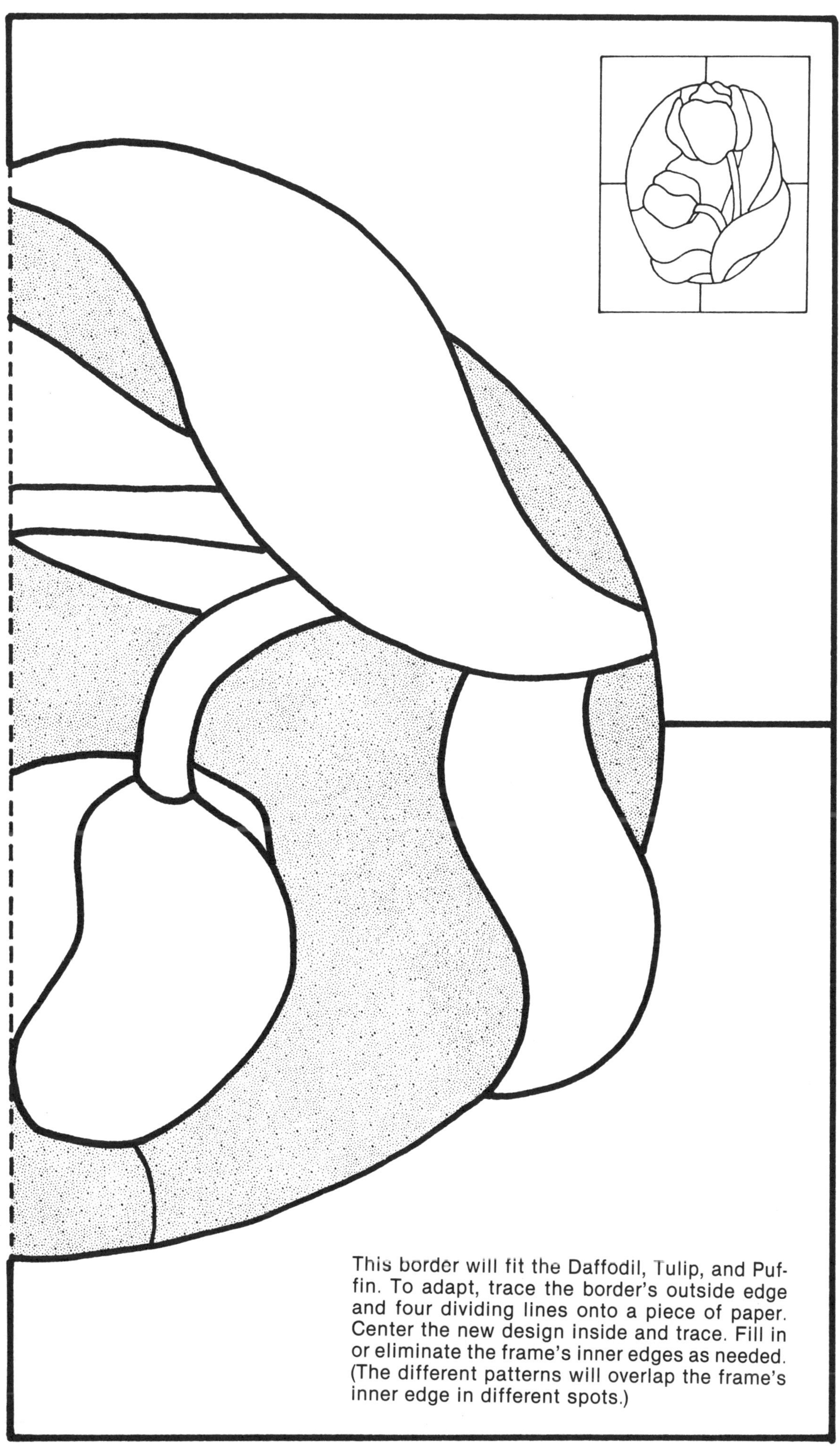

This border will fit the Daffodil, Tulip, and Puffin. To adapt, trace the border's outside edge and four dividing lines onto a piece of paper. Center the new design inside and trace. Fill in or eliminate the frame's inner edges as needed. (The different patterns will overlap the frame's inner edge in different spots.)

MERMAID

Dress up any powder room with this 24 piece beauty. This design is particularly striking when made of mostly irridescent glass. It gives a whole new look for nighttime viewing and also looks great on a mirror.

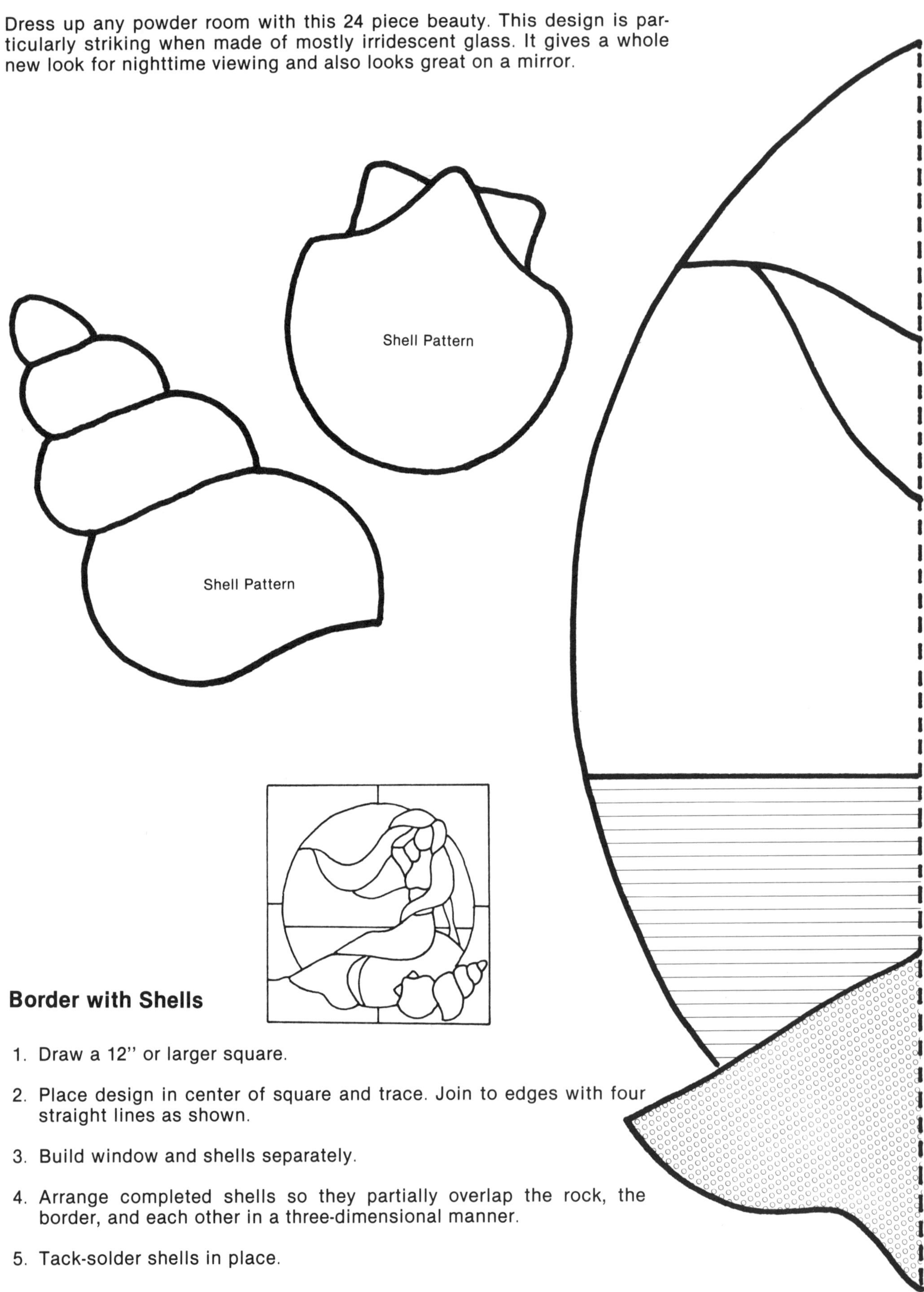

Border with Shells

1. Draw a 12" or larger square.

2. Place design in center of square and trace. Join to edges with four straight lines as shown.

3. Build window and shells separately.

4. Arrange completed shells so they partially overlap the rock, the border, and each other in a three-dimensional manner.

5. Tack-solder shells in place.

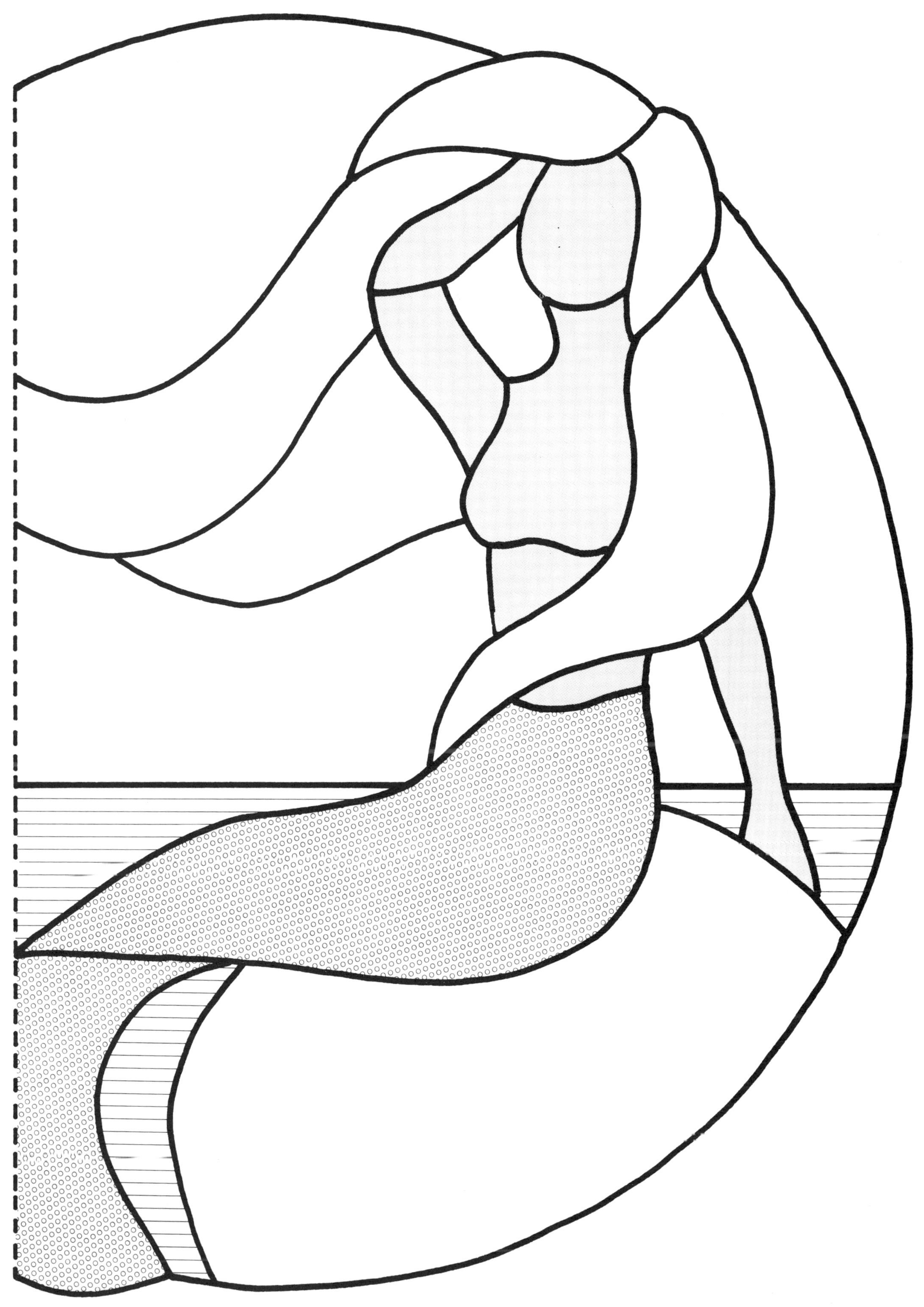

PUFFIN

A sea bird in real life, the Puffin is a natural for stained glass. It tops off its white and black feathers with a brilliant red-yellow-orange beak, red feet, and an adorable look in its eye. There are 23 pieces in this design.

Border Variations

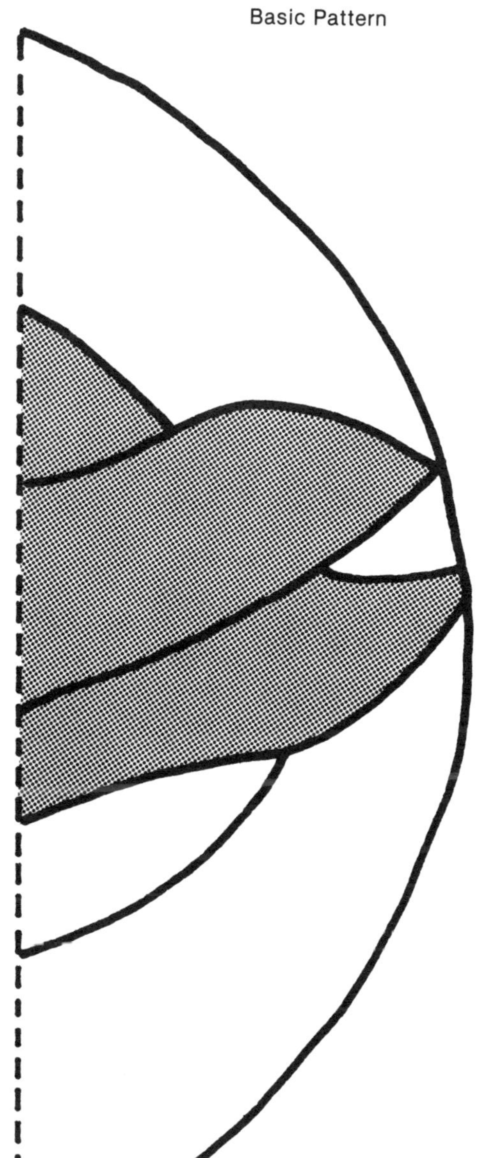

An Easy Puffin Eye

1. On the pattern, temporarily eliminate the eye and join the cheek lines so they run through the eye area. (Illustration A)

2. With scissors, cut eyelash shape from wide foil. Tin, then tack-solder base of eyelash only to cheek line. (Illustration B)

3. Cut a circle shape from wide foil and adhere it to a small white glass nugget to create the pupil of the eye. Wrap narrow foil around the entire edge of nugget, overlapping the edge of the circle piece. (Illustration C)

4. Tin the eye, then tack in place over bottom of eyelash piece and joining to cheek solder line. (Illustration D)

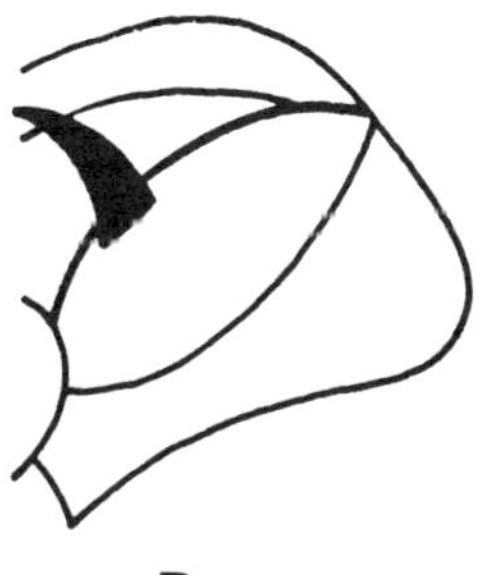

A

B

C

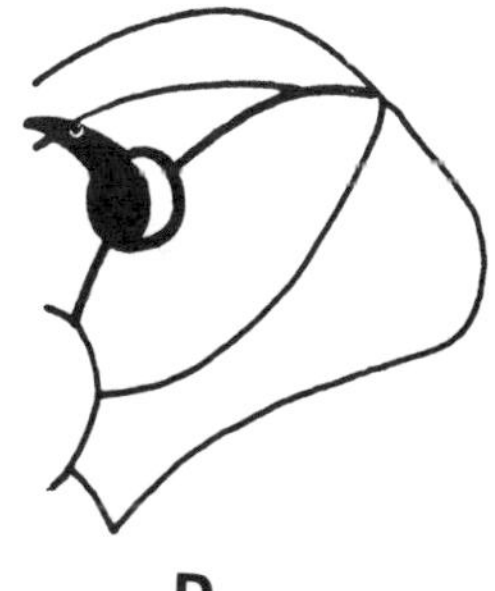

D

COUNTRY CHICKEN

This basic pattern has 20 pieces. Its' stylized country look
will go with many "unchickenlike" colors, so anything goes.

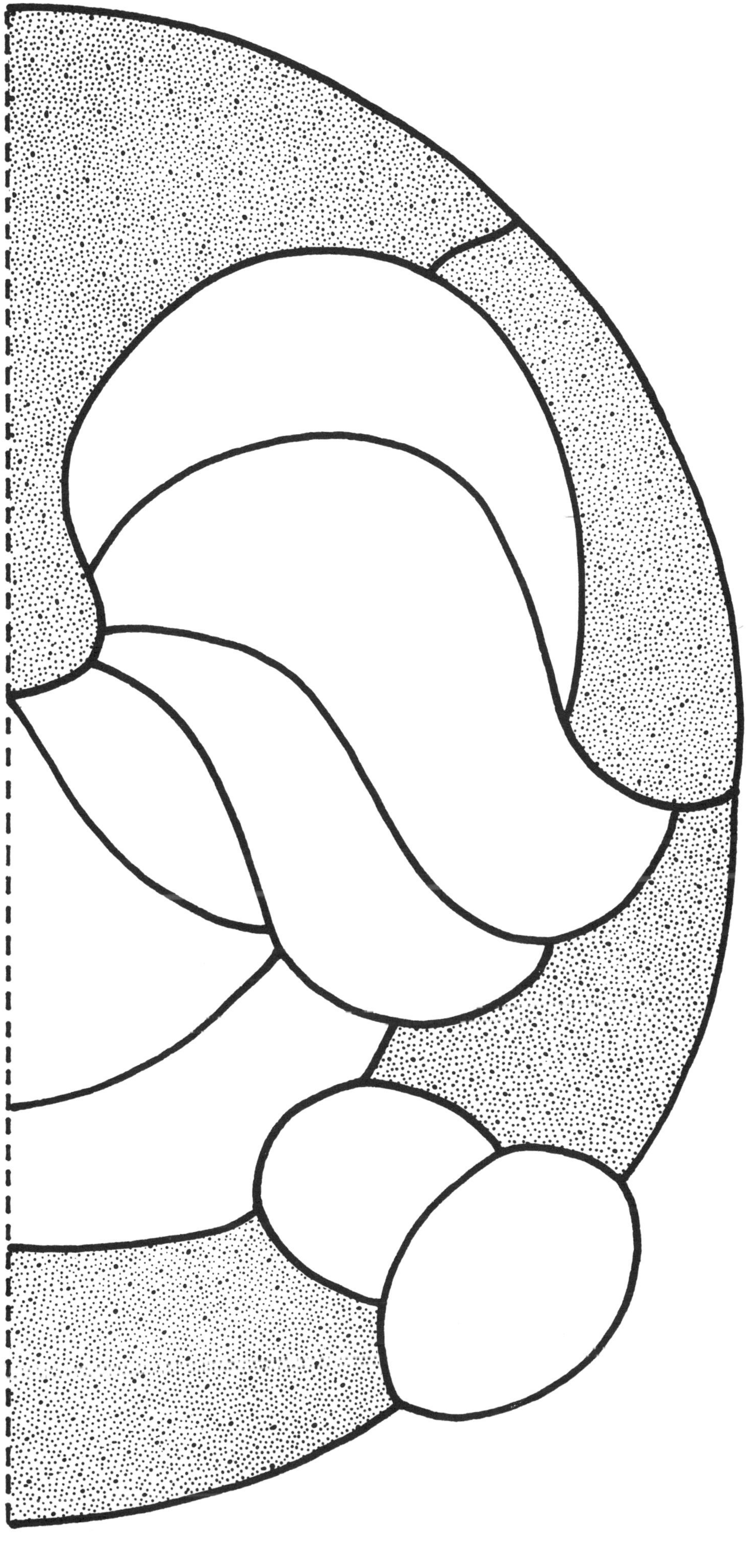

Border with Extra Eggs

1. Draw a 12'' or larger square.

2. Place design in center of square and trace. Join to edges with four straight lines as shown.

3. Build window. Cut, foil, and tin 3 to 5 extra eggs.

4. Arrange extra eggs so they partially overlap eggs in panel, the border, and each other in a three-dimensional manner.

5. Tack-solder the extra eggs in place.

FULL-SIZE PATTERNS

All of the designs in this book are available as full-size patterns. Check with your local stained glass dealer for purchase information. If not available, send check or money order for $6.00 per pattern (includes postage and handling) to:

CKE PUBLICATIONS
2840E Black Lake Blvd.
Olympia, WA 98502

Pattern Number	Title	Page Number	Size in Inches	Size in Centimeters
CKE-1	Flower Duet	6	12 + circles	30 + circles
CKE-2	Butterfly Duet	42	12 by 16	30 by 41
CKE-3	Flower Quartet	32	5 by 14 5/8	13 by 37
CKE-4	Driftwood	36	20 by 24	51 by 61
CKE-5	Classic Silhouette	30	12 by 20	30 by 51
CKE-6	Hot Air Balloons	38	18 by 24	46 by 61
CKE-7	Triple Tulips	26	16 circle	41 circle
CKE-8	Rose Bouquet	43	22 circle	56 circle
CKE-9	Birds with Roses	7	22 octagon	56 octagon
CKE-10	Dogwood and Hummingbird	32	22 octagon	56 octagon
CKE-11	Lake Scene	3	22 octagon	56 octagon
CKE-12	Nature's Beauty	3	17 3/8 by 28	44 by 71
CKE-13	Sailboat Duet	38	12 by 17	30 by 43
CKE-14	Double Rainbow	39	21½ by 14	55 by 36
CKE-15	Deer Portrait	35	19¼ by 25	49 by 63.5
CKE-16	Wagon Wheel	8	21¼ by 27½	54 by 70
CKE-17	Desert Sunrise	31	20 circle	51 circle
CKE-18	Sunrise on the Pond	37	20 by 28	51 by 71
CKE-19	Mallards in Flight	31	12 by 16	30 by 41
CKE-20	Dolphin and Whale	36	12 circle	30 circle
CKE-21	Geese	10	20 circle	51 circle
CKE-22	Bird and Flower	24	16 by 20	41 by 51
CKE-23	Koala Bear	18	18 by 24	46 by 61
CKE-24	Mare and Foal	8	30 3/4 by 22	78 by 56
CKE-25	Horse with Branches	33	20 circle	51 circle
CKE-26	Pheasant in Flight	29	22 by 22	56 by 56
CKE-27	Frog on Mushroom	47	20 circle	51 circle
CKE-28	Fish Jumping	35	16 by 20	41 by 51
CKE-29	Lilies	28	16 by 20	41 by 51
CKE-30	Sunny Daffodil	30	16 by 20	41 by 51

FULL-SIZE PATTERNS

Pattern Number	Title	Page Number	Size in Inches	Size in Centimeters
CKE-31	Sea Breeze	39	20½ circle	52 circle
CKE-32	Winter	20	28¼ by 17½	72 by 44
CKE-33	Farm Scene	9	21 circle	53 circle
CKE-34	Enchanted Tree	33	16¼ by 22	41 by 56
CKE-35	Feline Friends	17	20 circle	51 circle
CKE-36	Bear Fishing	34	19 3/4 by 25	50 by 63.5
CKE-37	Peeking Through	34	15 3/4 by 22 3/4	40 by 58
CKE-38	Mountain Lion	18	24 by 20	61 by 51
CKE-39	Unicorn with Rainbow	44	20 circle	51 circle
CKE-40	Birds and Flowers	24	12 by 12	30 by 30
CKE-41	Roses and Butterflies	4	16 by 16	41 by 41
CKE-42	Hummingbird Duet	7	12 by 16	30 by 41
CKE-43	Gladiola	6	20 by 26	51 by 66
CKE-44	Sweet Bouquet	5	18 circle	46 circle
CKE-45	Fruit Medley	4	18 circle	46 circle
CKE-46	Garden Prize	29	18 by 24	46 by 61
CKE-47	Iris Scene	18	14¼ by 28¼	36 by 72
CKE-48	Close-up	19	21 circle	53 circle
CKE-49	Mother and Child	46	15½ by 22½	39 by 57
CKE-50	Fun Forms	46	Bubbles 11¼ by 16 Waves 12 by 16	29 by 41 30 by 41
CKE-51	Mini Victorians	27	12 circle	12 circle
CKE-52	Formal Flower	27	32 3/4 by 16	83 by 41
CKE-53	Circle Floral	42	17 3/4 circle	45 circle
CKE-54	Bamboo and Calla Lillies	21	18 by 66	46 by 168
CKE-55	Sailboat Window	3	20 octagon	51 octagon
CKE-56	Bamboo Window	21	18 by 66	46 by 168
CKE-57	Fleur-de-lis	26	27½ by 20	70 by 51
CKE-58	Bird and Flower	28	20 octagon	51 octagon
CKE-59	Grape Oval	43	18 by 28½	45 by 72
CKE-60	Deer Window	35	21 by 66	53 by 168

FULL-SIZE PATTERNS

Pattern Number	Title	Page Number	Size in Inches	Size in Centimeters
CKE-61	Eagle in Flight	30	12 by 29¼	30 by 74
CKE-62	Gridwork Elegance	42	17¼ by 29½	144 by 75
CKE-63	Arched Floral	23	19 by 26	48 by 66
CKE-64	Love Bird	20	9 by 30	23 by 76
CKE-65	White Lilies	22	18 by 29	46 by 74
CKE-66	Dancer	47	22 by 34	56 by 86
CKE-67	Orchids	5	18 circle	46 circle
CKE-68	Calico and Tulips	16	28 by 34½	71 by 87
CKE-69	Rosebud Vase	22	10 by 30	25 by 67
CKE-70	Whale	37	22 by 22	56 by 56
CKE-71	Tulip Bowl	40	22 by 30	56 by 76
CKE-72	Prancin' Fancy	45	22½ by 22½	57 by 57
CKE-73	Castle in the Clouds	45	16 by 22½	41 by 57
CKE-74	Crescent Moon	15	20½ circle	52 circle
CKE-75	Baby Unicorn	13	21 by 23	53 by 58
CKE-76	Frick 'n Frack	20	25 by 34	63.5 by 86
CKE-77	Roller Balloons	44	23 by 26	58 by 66
CKE-78	Frog and Dragonfly	40	24 by 25	61 by 63.5
CKE-79	Floral Bowl	21	23 by 18	58 by 45
CKE-80	Vegetable	9	27 7/8 by 14	71 by 36
CKE-81	Four Pots	40	30 by 18	76 by 46
CKE-82	Orchid	32	16 by 26	41 by 51
CKE-83	Parrot	41	20 by 24	51 by 61
CKE-84	Peacock	25	30 by 37	76 by 94
CKE-85	Budding Beauty	23	26 by 20	66 by 51
CKE-86	Ducks in a Row	11	22¼ by 16	56.5 by 30.6
CKE-87	Rooster Reveille	11	23¼ by 24	59 by 61
CKE-88	Pig Jig	10	20 by 16¼	51 by 41.3
CKE-89	Mañana	12	21 by 20	53.3 by 51
CKE-90	Sittin' Pretty	12	13 by 18 3/4	33 by 47.6
	Frog Prince		15½ circle	39.4 circle
CKE-91	Cuddle Up Bears	14	22 by 16	55.9 by 40.9
CKE-92	C'Mon Out	17	16 by 25	40.6 by 63.5
CKE-93	Calla Lily	27	18 by 35	45.7 by 89
CKE-94	Bird of Paradise	41	31 by 21	78.7 by 53.3
CKE-95	Country Cousins	13	21 by 18	53.3 by 45.7
CKE-96	Joy Rides	14	16 by 20	40.6 by 51
CKE-97	Air Bear	15	16 by 24	40.6 by 61
CKE-98	Columbine and Friend	19	19½ by 23	49.5 by 58.4